U.S. Navy Special Forces

SEAL TEAMS

by Michael Burgan

CAPSTONE BOOKS
an imprint of Capstone Press
Mankato, Minnesota

Capstone Books are published by Capstone Press
151 Good Counsel Drive, P. O. Box 669, Mankato, Minnesota 56002
http://www.capstone-press.com

Library of Congress Cataloging-in-Publication Data
Burgan, Michael.
    U.S. Navy special forces: SEAL teams/by Michael Burgan.
    p. cm.—(Warfare and weapons)
    Includes bibliographical references (p. 44) and index.
    Summary: Introduces the Navy special forces known as SEALs, describing
their mission, history, and the equipment they use.
    ISBN 0-7368-0340-8
    1. United States. Navy. SEALS—Juvenile literature. 2. United States.
Navy—Commando troops—Juvenile literature. [1.United States. Navy. SEALs.
2. Special operations (Military science)] I. Title. II. Series.
VG87.B8697 2000
359.9—dc21   99-28600
                                                   CIP

Editorial Credits
Blake Hoena, editor; Timothy Halldin, cover designer; Linda Clavel, illustrator;
    Heidi Schoof, photo researcher

Photo Credits
Archive Photos, 12; Archive Photos/Agence France Presse, 18
Corbis, 14
Corbis/Bettmann, 16
Corbis/Jim Sugar Photography, 36
David Bohrer, 7, 8, 22, 25, 31
Photri-Microstock, 28, 32, 39, 43, 44, 46; Photri-Microstock/Robert Genat, cover, 4

**Special thanks to Naval Special Warfare Command Public Affairs for reviewing
this material, and to David Bohrer, Pulitzer Prize-winning photographer for the
Los Angeles Times, for providing interior photos.**

Table of Contents

Chapter 1

SEAL Teams

On the morning of October 25, 1983, members of SEAL Team Four approached a beach on Grenada. The beach on this Caribbean island was near Pearls Airfield. U.S. military commanders sent SEALs to scout the beach and airfield. The information they gathered would help U.S. military commanders decide whether to attack rebel forces there. These rebels had taken over the Grenadian government.

The SEALs traveled toward the beach on inflatable rafts. Once they were near the beach, two of the SEALs swam to shore. They would decide if it was safe for the rest of their team to come ashore.

SEALs often use inflatable rafts to sneak onto shore during missions.

At the time, rebel soldiers were on the beach preparing for an attack. But bad weather soon forced them to leave the beach and seek shelter. The two SEALs then signalled the rest of their team to come ashore. The SEALs quickly gathered the needed information and left the island.

The U.S. military's attack on Grenada began that same day. Several days later, the U.S. military defeated the Grenadian rebels.

Sea, Air, and Land

SEALs are specially trained members of the U.S. Navy. They perform high-risk missions that regular navy members are not trained to do. SEALs often perform target-designation and observation missions. During these missions, SEALs scout enemy forces and territory. SEALs perform search-and-rescue missions. They also perform precision-strike missions. During these missions, SEALs attack specific enemy targets. These targets may include enemy headquarters or weapons.

SEALs are specially trained members of the U.S. Navy.

SEALs train to work in water.

The U.S. Navy has six SEAL teams. SEAL Teams One, Three, and Five are stationed at the Naval Amphibious Base in Coronado, California. SEAL Teams Two, Four, and Eight are stationed in Little Creek, Virginia.

SEAL stands for sea, air, and land. SEALs are trained to work in water. They can climb aboard enemy ships without being seen or heard. SEALs learn to use parachutes. These large pieces of strong, light cloth allow SEALs to jump from aircraft and float slowly to the ground. SEALs also are trained to fight and perform missions on land.

SEAL team members often call themselves "quiet professionals." They do not talk about their missions. The government does not want enemies to know too much about SEAL teams. Most information about SEAL missions is classified. This secret information includes the size of the teams. It also includes missions they have performed recently or are planning to perform in the future.

Special Operations
SEAL teams are part of the U.S. military's Special Operations Forces. These forces often perform clandestine operations. These missions are secret. Regular military forces are not trained to perform them.

Some Special Operations Forces have duties other than those of navy SEALs. U.S. Air Force Pararescue teams are trained to perform search-and-rescue missions. They attempt to rescue pilots whose aircraft have crashed in enemy territory. U.S. Army Rangers often are sent to battle sites before the main U.S. forces arrive. Rangers scout enemy territory. They also may be assigned to capture enemy airfields. U.S. aircraft then use these airfields to carry troops and supplies to battle sites.

SEAL teams are an important part of the U.S. military's Special Operations Forces. SEALs can successfully complete missions while working secretly in small groups. They also work well with other Special Operations Forces. SEALs can be ready to perform missions anywhere in the world within 72 hours' notice.

Eagle: The bald eagle is a national symbol of the United States; it stands for freedom.

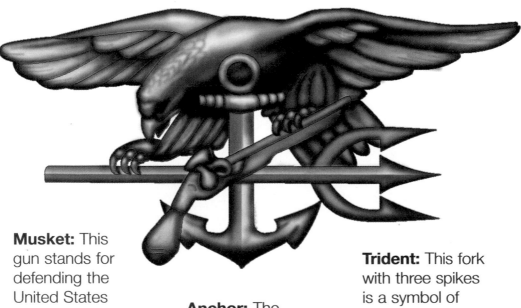

Musket: This gun stands for defending the United States and the freedom of its citizens.

Anchor: The anchor represents the U.S. Navy.

Trident: This fork with three spikes is a symbol of the sea.

Chapter 2

SEAL Teams' History

The history of the SEALs began during World War II (1939–1945). The Allied nations and the Axis powers fought this war. The Allied nations included the United States, Great Britain, Canada, and Russia. The Axis powers consisted of Germany, Italy, and Japan.

The Axis forces often placed mines and barricades along beaches. These obstacles prevented Allied boats from carrying troops to shore. The U.S. military needed soldiers who were trained to destroy the obstacles and guide attacking forces safely ashore. These soldiers were trained to perform many of their duties in

The U.S. military needed soldiers specially trained to help safely guide Allied boats ashore.

The navy trained UDTs to sneak ashore and map the beaches on islands held by the Japanese.

the water. Some of these duties were similar to those performed by SEALs today.

Scouts and Raiders

The U.S. military established Scout and Raider units during World War II. These soldiers were trained to support amphibious landings. During amphibious landings, boats carried soldiers from ships at sea to the shore. Enemy forces often placed obstacles in the water and on beaches. These objects made amphibious landings difficult. Scout and Raider units were trained to destroy these obstacles.

In 1942, a Scout and Raider team performed its first mission during Operation Torch. This operation began the United States' invasion of Africa. The military sent a Scout and Raider team to cut cables supporting an anti-shipping net. This net blocked a river and prevented U.S. warships from sailing upstream. Under enemy fire, the Scout and Raider team successfully completed its mission.

Underwater Demolition Teams

During World War II, the navy also developed Underwater Demolition Teams (UDTs). Many UDTs worked in the Pacific Ocean. U.S. forces in the Pacific region were fighting the Japanese. The Japanese controlled many small islands near and around Japan. UDT members swam ashore before attacks took place on these islands. They made maps of the beaches and any obstacles blocking beaches. For example, coral reefs often prevented U.S. ships from

reaching the shore. UDTs blew up anything that blocked the path for U.S. ships and boats.

UDTs served again during the Korean War (1950–1953). During this war, they rarely swam ashore as they performed missions. Instead, they worked secretly in enemy territory. UDTs blew up bridges and railroads. They also cleared mines from harbors. Mines are floating devices that explode when ships sail into them.

The Birth of the SEALs

In 1961, the United States was involved in the Vietnam War (1954–1975). President John F. Kennedy decided the U.S. military needed to strengthen its special forces. These forces were trained in unconventional warfare. They could secretly operate in enemy territory. They also could spy on enemy camps, blow up bridges, or perform rescue missions. Much of the fighting during the Vietnam War was unconventional.

The U.S. Navy created SEAL Teams One and Two for unconventional warfare. SEAL Team One was based in Little Creek, Virginia. SEAL Team Two was based in Coronado, California.

Unconventional warfare often involves sneaking into enemy territory.

During the Vietnam War, the United States supported the South Vietnamese against the North Vietnamese.

These SEALs trained in hand-to-hand combat, foreign languages, parachuting, and demolitions. They learned to use explosives to destroy objects such as bridges. The SEAL teams also included many UDT members. UDT members already had experience and training in unconventional warfare.

In 1962, the navy sent SEALs to Vietnam. The United States supported the South

Vietnamese against the North Vietnamese in this war. At first, SEALs were sent to train South Vietnamese soldiers in unconventional warfare. Later, SEALs attacked enemy camps and cut radio lines. Many of their attacks helped stop the movement of enemy troops and supplies.

Grenada

In 1983, SEAL teams took part in Operation Urgent Fury. The United States sent troops to Grenada during this operation. These troops were sent to protect U.S. medical students there. Rebels had taken over the government on Grenada. The U.S. government thought the rebels might endanger the medical students.

SEAL teams took part in several missions during Operation Urgent Fury. SEALs scouted out the Salines Airport on Grenada. They gathered information about the airport's runways and enemy forces there. Other SEALs protected the governor-general of Grenada from rebel forces.

Mission

Operation: Urgent Fury

Date: October 25, 1983

Location: Grenada

Situation: The U.S. military sent members of a SEAL team to take control of the Radio Free Grenada radio transmitter near St. George's. This transmitter was capable of sending information about the U.S. attack throughout the Caribbean region.

Transmitter: Two Blackhawk helicopters dropped the SEALs off near the transmitter. The SEALs quickly overpowered the guards at the radio station and took control of it.

Counterattack: Rebel soldiers heard of the attack on the radio station. They began a counterattack. The rebels outnumbered the SEALs. They also had more powerful weapons. The rebels had a mortar. They used this cannon to fire small bombs at the SEALs. The rebels also had an Armored Personnel Carrier. This troop-carrying vehicle had a machine gun mounted on it.

Escape: Four SEALs were wounded during the counterattack. The SEALs decided they could not defend the transmitter against the rebel forces. They chose to blow it up instead. The SEALs then escaped to the nearby sea where a navy ship waited for them.

20

Kilometers
0 1 2 3

Miles
0 1 2

☆ **Capital**
○ City

*Caribbean
Sea*

Pearls ○

GRENADA

☆ **St. George's**

*Atlantic
Ocean*

North
America

*Atlantic
Ocean*

*Pacific
Ocean*

South
America

Chapter 3

Training
for Battle

Becoming a SEAL team member is not easy. All SEALs must go through several months of hard physical and mental training.

BUD/S Training

All SEALs are volunteers. They are members of the Navy who have asked to serve with the SEALs. These volunteers must pass a written and physical test before entering SEAL training.

Only men can become SEALs. Congressional law does not allow women to enter ground combat specialties. These jobs may involve duties that are performed while under direct fire from enemy forces.

SEALs must be physically fit.

The first part of SEAL training is called Basic Underwater Demolition/SEAL (BUD/S). BUD/S training lasts about six months. It is some of the most difficult physical training in any of the U.S. armed forces. About seven out of every 10 trainees drop out of BUD/S.

BUD/S training takes place at the Naval Special Warfare Center in Coronado, California. BUD/S starts with physical training. Trainees swim as much as five miles (8 kilometers) at a time. They jog as far as 14 miles (23 kilometers). They spend many hours doing physical exercises. These exercises include push-ups, sit-ups, and jumping jacks.

After four weeks of BUD/S, trainees reach "Hell Week." This is the most difficult part of their training. They train for five days in a row with almost no sleep. Trainees are constantly forced to do physical exercises and perform training exercises. This training tests the trainees' physical and mental limits.

SEALs spend a great deal of time training in the water.

Additional Training

The next part of BUD/S focuses on diving. SEALs practice using different types of Scuba gear. Scuba stands for "self-contained underwater breathing apparatus." The air tanks and masks in this gear allow swimmers to breathe underwater. The ability to work underwater separates SEALs from most other U.S. Special Operations Forces.

Trainees then learn how to work on land. They practice firing many kinds of weapons. They also use different explosives. SEAL trainees learn patrolling and rappelling techniques. Rappelling is a method of using ropes to climb down mountains and hillsides.

Next, trainees go through the final stages of training. They learn how to parachute. Trainees also receive basic medical training. They need to know how to treat minor injuries.

After finishing training, trainees are then sent to a SEAL team to train further. They train for at least six more months with a SEAL team before they are considered SEALs.

Military Terms

ASDS – Advanced SEAL Delivery System; this vehicle is a submarine.

Blow and Go – a diving term for exiting a submarine

BUD/S – Basic Underwater Demolition/SEAL training

CRRC – Compact Rubber Raiding Craft; CRRCs are also called Zodiacs.

GPS – Global Positioning System; this system can tell SEALs their exact location anywhere in the world.

HAHO – High Altitude, High Opening; a type of parachute jump in which jumpers open their parachutes high above the ground.

HALO – High Altitude, Low Opening; a type of parachute jump in which jumpers open their parachutes close to the ground.

Hop and Pop – a term referring to when a SEAL jumps out of an aircraft and immediately starts to fire his weapon

PBR – Patrol Boat, Riverine

RIB – Rigid-Hull Inflatable Boat

SCUBA – Self-Contained Underwater Breathing Apparatus

SDV – SEAL Delivery Vehicle; this vehicle is a wet submarine.

Chapter 4

Weapons of War

SEAL teams use many different kinds of equipment. Some of these tools are common. SEALs may carry flashlights, pocket knives, and matches. But SEALs also use some special weapons such as machine guns.

SEALs also may use different types of watercraft on their missions. Some of these craft are boats. Some are tiny submarines. These watercraft help SEALs move quickly and quietly to their mission sites.

Machine Guns and Rifles

SEALs carry weapons to protect themselves. The MP-5 is a common weapon that SEALs use. The MP-5 is a German submachine gun. These lightweight guns can fire many bullets

SEALs use different types of watercraft and weapons during missions.

quickly. The MP-5 also works well after being carried through water.

Many SEALs use M-4 carbine-automatic rifles. The M-4 is one of the most common rifles used by SEALs. These rifles can fire bullets rapidly.

SEAL snipers use other rifles. Snipers are trained to hit distant targets with a single bullet. Sniper rifles include the M-14 and the M-88.

On and Under the Water

SEAL team members use many different watercraft. One of these is the Patrol Boat, Riverine (PBR). The PBR was first used during the Vietnam War. The PBR is designed to move through very shallow water. It also is designed to change direction very quickly. The PBR carries machine guns and a grenade launcher. Grenades are small explosives.

The Mark V Special Operations Craft is the newest watercraft used by SEAL teams. This boat can travel at speeds of more than 50 miles

Snipers are trained to hit distant targets.

The SDV is a wet submarine that transports SEALs to mission sites.

(80 kilometers) per hour. It also can carry as many as 16 SEALs to a mission site.

SEALs often come ashore on small watercraft. One such boat is the Rigid-Hull Inflatable Boat (RIB). This boat moves well through rough waters. The Combat Rubber

Raiding Craft (CRRC) is another such boat. The CRRC is powered by a small outboard engine. SEALs also can quietly row this boat to shore. The CRRC can be launched from a larger boat, a helicopter, or a submarine.

SEALs use small submarines to move underwater. The SEAL Delivery Vehicle (SDV) is a wet submarine. The inside of the submarine is filled with water. SEALs wear scuba gear as they travel in this submarine. SEALs can use SDVs to reach mission sites secretly.

The newest SEAL submarine is the Advanced SEAL Delivery System (ASDS). The ASDS is a dry submarine. SEALs do not need to wear scuba gear inside the submarine. This vehicle allows SEALs to rest and stay dry while approaching mission sites.

Electronic Tools

SEAL teams use electronic equipment on their missions. Some of these devices help SEALs communicate with each other and their commanders. SEALs use radios with earpieces and microphones that are strapped to their heads. This allows them to talk and keep their hands free. Other radios send signals to satellites. These spacecraft orbit the earth. SEALs use these radios to communicate over long distances.

The Global Positioning System (GPS) is another important electronic tool. The GPS looks like a small calculator. This device uses radio signals from satellites to let SEALs know their location anywhere on Earth. The GPS helps SEALs locate their mission sites.

Important Dates

1939 – World War II begins

1942 – Operation Torch; a Scout and Raider team cuts an anti-shipping net during the U.S invasion of Africa.

1950 – Korean War begins; UDTs blow up Korean bridges and railroads and remove mines from harbors.

1954 – Vietnam War begins

1962 – First SEAL teams form

1966 – Patrol Boats, Riverine first used

1983 – Operation Urgent Fury; SEAL teams perform several missions during the U.S. invasion of Grenada.

1989 – Operation Just Cause; SEAL teams are sent to Panama to help capture General Manuel Noriega.

1990 – Gulf War begins

1995 – Mark V Special Operations Craft first used

Late 1990s – Introduction of the Advanced SEAL Delivery System

Chapter 5

The Present and the Future

SEAL teams will continue to be needed in the future. Their training helps them perform many special missions. SEAL teams also help train special operations forces in other countries. Some SEALs help inform the public about the navy and SEAL teams.

Leap Frogs

Leap Frogs are the navy's parachute-demonstration team. This team is made up of members from several of the SEAL teams. Leap Frogs perform parachute jumps for public audiences around the United States.

Leap Frogs show the public the high level of skill needed to be a navy SEAL. Members of

The SEAL parachute-demonstration team performs for public audiences.

the parachute team also answer questions about parachuting and the navy. They even sign autographs.

Special Operations

Some military leaders believe there will be no major wars in the future. They believe the United States may perform more special operations missions. SEALs will be needed for these missions.

SEALs are an important part of the U.S. Navy. Recently, they have performed special operations missions in Bosnia, Somalia, Haiti, and Liberia. SEAL teams are prepared to perform missions anywhere in the world.

SEALs will be needed for special operations missions in the future.

Words to Know

clandestine operation (KLAN-des-tuhn op-uh-RAY-shuhn)—secret mission performed by SEALs

classified information (KLASS-uh-fide in-fur-MAY-shuhn)—information that is kept secret

demolitions (dem-oh-LISH-uhns)—the use of explosives to destroy objects

Global Positioning System (GLOH-buhl puh-ZI-shuh-ning SISS-tuhm)—an electronic tool used to find the location of a person or object anywhere on Earth

grenade (gruh-NADE)—a small bomb; some types of this explosive device can be thrown by soldiers and other types can be fired from a grenade launcher.

mine (MINE)—an explosive device that floats in the water and explodes when a ship sails into it

parachute (PA-ruh-shoot)—a piece of strong, lightweight fabric; people use parachutes to safely jump from aircraft.

rebel (REB-uhl)—a person who fights against the ruling government

satellite (SAT-uh-lite)—a spacecraft that orbits Earth

scout (SKOUT)—a person sent to collect information about enemy forces

sniper (SNI-puhr)—a shooter trained to hit distant targets

To Learn More

Bohrer, David. *America's Special Forces.* Osceola, Wis.: MBI Publishing, 1998.

Green, Michael. *River Patrol Boats.* Land and Sea. Mankato, Minn.: Capstone Books, 1999.

Halberstadt, Hans. *U.S. Navy SEALs in Action.* Osceola, Wis.: Motorbooks International, 1995.

Streissguth, Tom. *U.S. Navy SEALs.* Serving Your Country. Minneapolis: Capstone Press, 1996.

Tomajczyk, Stephen F. *U.S. Elite Counter-Terrorist Forces.* Osceola, Wis.: Motorbooks International, 1997.

Useful Addresses

Naval Special Warfare Center
Naval Amphibious Base Coronado
San Diego, CA 92118

UDT SEAL Museum
3300 N A1A North Hutchinson Island
Fort Pierce, FL 34949

Internet Sites

Naval Special Warfare Command
http://www.navsoc.navy.mil

Navy SEALs
http://www.chinfo.navy.mil/navpalib/factfile/
  personnel/seals/seals.html

Special Operations.Com
http://www.specialoperations.com

Special Operations Command Europe
http://www.eucom.mil/hq/soceur/index.htm

U.S. Navy Online
http://www.navy.mil

Index